Cornerstones of Freedom

The Pony Express

Peter Anderson

CHILDREN'S PRESS®
A Division of Grolier Publishing
New York • London • Hong Kong • Sydney
Danbury, Connecticut

Library of Congress Cataloging-in-Publication Data

Anderson, Peter
   The Pony Express / by Peter Anderson.
      p. cm.—(Cornerstones of freedom)
   Includes index.
   Summary: Examines the establishment of this innovative but
short-lived mail delivery system and recounts anecdotes about it.
   ISBN 0-516-20002-X
   1. Pony express—History—Juvenile literature. 2. Postal service—
United States—History—Juvenile literature. 3. West (U.S.)—
History—1860–1890—Juvenile literature. [1. Pony express—History.
2. Postal service—History.] I. Title. II. Series.
HE6375.P65A53 1996
383'.143'0973—dc20

                                           96-2088
                                              CIP
                                               AC

"Wanted: Young, skinny, wiry fellows not over 18," read the newspaper advertisement. "Must be expert riders willing to risk death daily. Orphans preferred. Wages: $25.00 a week." One hundred dollars a month was a reasonable wage back in 1860, but it was hardly enough to compensate a young man for the risks he would face as a Pony Express rider.

In the spring of 1860, eighty young men were hired to carry the U.S. mail along a 1,966-mile (3,164-km) route between St. Joseph, Missouri, and Sacramento, California. Each rider carried the mail along a section of the route, changing horses about every 15 miles (24 km) to keep up speed. After 75 to 100 miles (120 to 161 km) of hard riding, he passed his mail pouch on to the next man.

This cross-country relay was a grueling routine. A rider might have to buck the winds on the prairies of Kansas and Nebraska, ford the Sweetwater River in Wyoming when it ran high in the spring, traverse the deserts of Utah and Nevada under a scorching sun, or dodge snowslides in California's Sierra Nevada Mountains. The Pony Express route ran through some of the most rugged and remote territory in the American West.

Brave men were willing to take the dangerous risk of being Pony Express riders (opposite page).

Stories of previous attempts to carry the mail between Salt Lake City, Utah, and California suggested that success was anything but certain. In May 1851, Major George Chorpenning Jr. and Absalom Woodward set out from Sacramento, California, their pack mules loaded down with the eastbound mail. On the way to Salt Lake City, Woodward was killed by American Indians. Chorpenning's wounds were so severe that he was unable to make the return trip to California.

Less than a year later, in February 1852, one of Chorpenning's employees left Sacramento with four other men and a team of pack mules. After their animals froze to death, the five men carried the mail on their backs through many miles of deep drifting snow. It took them fifty-three days in all to make the trip to Salt Lake City.

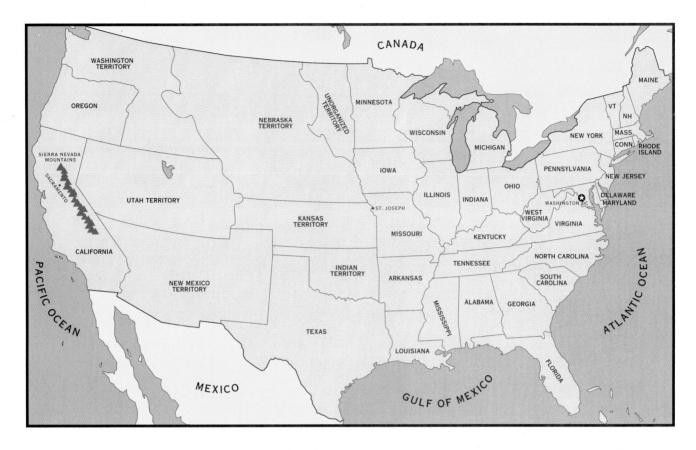

The United States and its territories in 1860

The odds were stacked against the Pony Express from the beginning. Nevertheless, William H. Russell, chief promoter of the Pony Express, had been able to convince his business partners, William B. Waddell and Alexander Majors, to join him in investing in this risky venture.

If anyone had the experience to set up a more efficient mail service, it was Russell, Majors, and Waddell. For years they had run one of America's most successful overland freight businesses. They owned thousands of oxen and wooden wagons, which they used to haul freight across the Great Plains to the Rocky Mountains and beyond.

William H. Russell (right), Alexander Majors (middle), and William B. Waddell (far right) were adventurous businessmen.

It was the flamboyant Russell who had often taken on the role of promoter and fund-raiser for the freighting company. He had been successful in his efforts, but there had been failures as well. Majors and Waddell were more cautious and practical than their partner, and they had bailed Russell out of several bad business decisions. They believed that the risks were high with the Pony Express, but it was too late to back out. Russell had already invested in the new mail route. He further jeopardized his company's reputation when he promised that the Pony Express would deliver the mail to California in ten days or less.

Two thousand miles (3,218 km) in ten days or less? It took John Butterfield's Stage Line at least twice that long to get the mail to California. It was true that the Butterfield route was less direct—it swung along a great arc that curved down through Texas, New Mexico, and what are now Arizona and Nevada before curling up into southern California. But it was also farther south. Winters along that

This advertisement for the Pony Express told its New York customers how fast their letters could reach the West Coast.

The Butterfield Stage Line carried mail to California, but the Pony Express riders were planning to take a shorter route.

well-traveled stagecoach route were less severe than in the north.

Since 1858, Butterfield's company had been receiving $600,000 a year from the U.S. government to make deliveries semimonthly to and from California. If the young riders of the Pony Express could deliver the mail in half the time it took Butterfield, shouldn't they get the mail contract? That's what Russell was counting on.

For years, William M. Gwin, a senator from California, had been lobbying Congress for better mail service to and from his state. Freighters like Benjamin F. Ficklin had insisted that a central route through Utah, Nevada, and the high Sierra Nevada Mountains would be quicker than Butterfield's stage route. As far as Russell was concerned, the only way to get the government behind a new mail route was to build a reputation for the Pony Express. And it would have to be done in a hurry. Without government support, the new mail service would surely lose money.

On April 3, 1860, an enthusiastic crowd gathered in the dusty streets of St. Joseph, Missouri, to bear witness to the beginning of William Russell's great scheme. The westbound mail was to arrive by locomotive, and a rider named John (Johnnie) Frye waited to start the first leg of the Pony Express on his pony. Decked out in flowered leggings and jingling plated spurs, young Johnnie Frye looked more like a circus rider than a mail carrier. Onlookers seeking souvenirs crowded around his pony. They plucked so many horsehairs for mementos, that one reporter said, "The little pony was almost robbed of its tail."

Johnnie Frye, the first Pony Express rider

So far, it seemed, Russell had succeeded in his role as a promoter for the Pony Express. When the train carrying the westbound mail arrived late, it only added to the drama that he hoped would capture the imagination of the American people. A determined engineer had stoked the fire on the locomotive and roared down the final stretch of tracks into St. Joseph. But his efforts were not enough to make up for time already lost. The Pony Express had yet to leave town, and the train was already two and a half hours behind schedule.

Finally, at 7:15 P.M., ceremonial shots from a brass cannon echoed through the streets. Carrying the westbound mail, Johnnie Frye spurred his mare and galloped through town to

A Pony Express rider leaves St. Joseph, Missouri.

the banks of the Missouri River, where a ferryboat awaited him. A half-hour boat ride to the town of Elmwood, Kansas, gave him time to change out of the fancy duds his boss had made him wear and into clothes better suited for trail riding.

From Elmwood, Frye followed a trail hard-packed from the hooves of oxen and the wheels of freight wagons. Even in the darkness, he had little trouble staying on the well-traveled route they called the Oregon Trail. Onward, across the dark prairie, he spurred his mare.

The Oregon Trail was a well-traveled route to the West. Ruts from the covered wagons still mark the ground today.

Meanwhile, another Pony Express rider, Sam Hamilton, was getting ready to leave Sacramento, California, with the eastbound mail. Two days of rain had turned California's roads into rivers of mud. As Hamilton rode through empty streets several hours after midnight, sheets of rain continued to wash through the night. Somehow he was able to cover the first 20 miles (32 km) to Folsom, California, in fifty-nine minutes, even though he switched horses three times.

But beyond Folsom, the road got even worse. Hamilton leaned forward in the saddle to help his horse up a steep hill, and leaned back as they came down the other side. Three times his horse fell to the ground. Three times he climbed back into the saddle and spurred her on to Placerville, California.

As the sky began to light up in the east, rain turned to hail. The steep trail turned slick. Once again his horse lost her footing. This time Hamilton hit the ground hard, slashing his cheek on the sharp edge of a boulder. Rising up out of the muck, he grabbed his pouch of mail from his saddle and ran up to the next station. There a fresh horse awaited him. Less than three minutes after his fall, he was back in the saddle and headed up the icy trail to Sportsman's Hall, California.

It was 6:48 A.M., April 4, when Hamilton arrived at the station at Sportsman's Hall. He had ridden through 60 miles (97 km) of rain and sleet, changed horses eight times, and gained 4,000 feet (1,219 m) in elevation. Soaked and bloody, he handed over his mailbag to Warren Upson, the next rider.

"Rough trip, Sam?" asked Upson.

" 'Twan't half bad," Hamilton replied.

Hamilton may have been reluctant to admit it, but it had been a rough night. Still, it wasn't half as rough as Upson's trek up and over the crest of the Sierra Nevada Mountains would prove to be. Upson's section of the trail was as treacherous as any along the Pony Express route, especially when the weather turned bad. As swirling snow piled into 30-foot (9-m) drifts, few

Upson had to trek over the Sierra Nevada Mountains during a blinding snowstorm.

landmarks could be seen that day. By the time Upson approached the summit of the Sierras, visibility was next to nothing. Fierce winds whipped drifting snow into a blinding white cloud. Upson led his horse, one small step at a time, knowing that a slight miscalculation might send them tumbling down the side of the mountain.

Somehow, despite these formidable obstacles, Upson and the other young riders, traveling non-stop night and day, were able to complete this first journey of the Pony Express. More amazingly, they were able to complete it on time. It would take thirty riders to bring the westbound mail into Sacramento. There, William (Billy) Hamilton, the last of the westbound riders, was met with a hero's welcome.

"First a cloud of rolling dust . . . then a horseman, and then a straggling, charging band of horsemen flying after him," was how a reporter for the *Sacramento Union* described Hamilton's arrival. "A cannon, placed on the square at J Street, sent forth its noisy welcome. Amidst the firing and shouting, and waving of hats and ladies handkerchiefs, the pony was seen coming down J Street, surrounded by about thirty citizens. Out of this confusion emerged the Pony Express, trotting up to the door of the agency and depositing its mail. . . . Hip, hip, hurrah for the Pony Carrier!"

When the eastbound mail arrived in Missouri a few hours later, a similar celebration took place in the streets of St. Joseph. Russell had plenty of reason to join in the festivities. Newspaper editors throughout the region were singing the praises of the Pony Express. They knew that better mail service would almost certainly increase business opportunities for Westerners. Russell hoped to ride this wave of publicity and popularity all the way to a government contract. But Congress, it seemed, was in no hurry to make a move. To get Congress's approval and support, he could only demand the utmost from his riders and hope for the best.

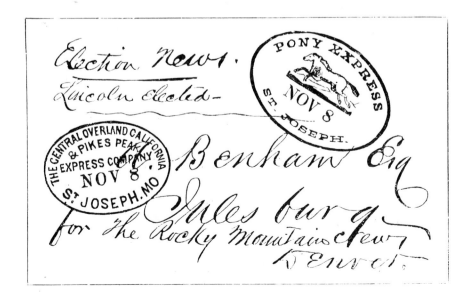

The Pony Express brought the East and West closer together. This letter shared the exciting news of Lincoln's election in 1860.

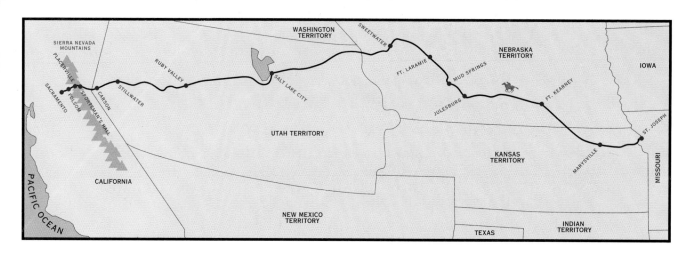

The route of the Pony Express ran from Missouri, through the Kansas, Nebraska, and Utah territories, to California. This region includes the present-day states of Kansas, Nebraska, Colorado, Wyoming, Utah, and Nevada.

Speed and endurance were essential for the Pony Express rider, not only to keep up with the demands of a tight schedule, but also to avoid encounters with roaming bands of American Indians. Many Paiute Indians, whose homelands covered much of present-day Utah and Nevada, resented white immigrants who were killing too many antelope and cutting down nut-bearing piñon pine trees. The Paiutes depended on these food sources. After an especially brutal winter that had taken many lives, some Paiutes were prepared to battle the immigrants, if that's what it would take to defend their livelihood.

One Paiute leader named Numaga argued for peace, but on May 7, 1860, a few young men defied his counsel. They raided the Williams Station of the Pony Express and killed five men. In the following weeks and months, many innocent people, both American Indians and immigrants, were attacked and killed. As one Pony Express rider found out, many people shot first and asked questions later.

*Paiute leader
Numaga*

J. G. Kelley rode one of the most desolate stretches of the Pony Express route in Nevada. One day he saw a wagon train up ahead. As he approached this caravan he heard shots. Why were the passengers of this wagon train shooting at him? He had no intention of slowing down long enough to find out. As it was, he was barely able to dodge their gunfire.

When he met the same caravan on his return trip, he approached their wagon train with caution. This time, however, the guns were silent. Kelley demanded an explanation for their previous attack on him. "We thought you were an Indian," came the reply.

A rider heading east waves to a wagon train heading west.

A Pony Express rider's best defense was his ability to travel faster and farther than anyone who had bad intentions. From his seat on a Nevada stagecoach, writer Mark Twain described the sight of an Express rider at work.

"Here he comes!" Twain wrote as the distant rider approached. "Away across the endless dead level of the prairie a black speck appears against the sky. . . In a second it becomes a horse and rider, rising and falling, rising and falling—sweeping toward us nearer and nearer . . . still nearer and the flutter of the

Writer Mark Twain

hoofs come faintly to the ear—another instant a whoop and a hurrah from our upper deck, a wave of the rider's hand . . . [Then] man and horse burst past like a belated fragment of storm."

To ride like that, Pony Expressmen had to travel light. A horse's load was limited to around 165 pounds (75 kg). Most riders were short and lean to begin with, weighing about 125 pounds (57 kg). They rarely carried any more than 20 pounds (9 kg) of mail. That left about 25 pounds (11 kg) for a saddle and anything else a rider chose to bring along.

Each rider carried a blanketlike leather mail pouch called a mochila (or mochilla), which he draped across his saddle. For self-defense, most riders settled on a single pistol. Sometimes they brought along an extra loaded cylinder. But Pony Expressmen used their weapons only in the most dire situations, which the best of horses helped them avoid.

"Uncle" Nick Wilson, a mail carrier who had grown up with the Shoshone Indians, spoke well of the horses he rode with the Pony Express. He recalled a time when some Paiute Indians jumped him in the high desert country of western Utah.

A mochila draped over a saddle

Pony Express riders often needed a gun for defense.

18

"I looked back over my shoulder," he said, "and saw them coming . . . as hard as they could ride after me, yellin' and shootin'." Wilson spurred the flanks of his horse and managed to stay out in front of the oncoming Indian ponies until they tired and fell back behind him.

What saved him, perhaps more than his horse's speed, was its endurance. The difference, Wilson believed, was in the horse's feed. Better feed made stronger muscles. He claimed that the grass-fed Indian ponies just couldn't keep up with the grain-fed horses belonging to the Pony Express.

Shipping in grain from Iowa farms to feed Pony Express horses took money. And the horses themselves had not come cheap. For a rider to make good time, he needed a fresh horse every 10 to 15 miles (16 to 24 km). As many as five hundred high-grade horses had been purchased and stabled at one hundred and twenty relay stations along the route.

A rider switches horses at a relay station.

19

An old Pony Express office in Gothenburg, Nebraska still stands (above). A plaque marks the sight of the Mud Springs Station in Nebraska (right).

At the Salt Lake House in Salt Lake City, Utah, Pony Express riders often stopped for the night. It had a reputation of entertaining a rough crowd.

Besides eighty young riders who carried the mail, as many as four hundred station men were hired. These were the men who maintained the lonely outposts along the Pony Express route. They made sure that replacement horses were ready and waiting when Pony Express riders came galloping into view.

The Pony Express was, by all accounts, a costly venture. And without government support, the Pony Express proved to be a losing proposition. Even at the relatively high rate of fifteen dollars an ounce, money gained from the delivery of the mail to and from California would never pay for the costs of running the business. Each day of mail service added to the debts already mounting up for Russell, Majors, and Waddell.

Worsening relations with the Paiutes led to further losses. By the end of May, the Paiutes had raided and destroyed seven relay stations, killing sixteen station hands and driving off one hundred and fifty horses. Unless the U.S. Army could offer his employees some protection, Alexander Majors said that the Pony Express would be forced to shut down.

On May 31, 1860, the Pony Express discontinued service. It wasn't until several stagecoaches were attacked that the army finally responded to Majors's plea. Troops were sent in, and they drove the Paiutes into the mountains of Nevada. There, the Paiutes suffered great losses when a late summer snowstorm swept through the high country. For the Paiutes, it was yet another crisis brought on by the white man's presence.

The army's success renewed William Russell's hopes for the Pony Express, which resumed

With the discovery of gold in California, many wagon trains of immigrants headed West, and settled in lands belonging to American Indians.

service on June 26. Still, money problems remained. Operation of the mail service continued to drain the cash reserves of the freighting company. And the freighting company had troubles of its own. A herd of freight oxen, valued at $150,000, had frozen to death during a blizzard near the Ruby Valley in Nevada. Worse, the U.S. War Department had been unable to pay a huge debt for freighting services provided during the winter of 1857–1858.

Buffalo Bill Cody rode for the Pony Express (above). He later became a famous entertainer (below).

The odds were mounting against Russell's high-stakes gamble. As he struggled to finance the operation, Pony Express riders continued to earn their reputation for courageous service in the face of grave dangers. One of those riders, a wiry lad soon to turn fifteen, rode an especially treacherous route in Wyoming. As if three whitewater crossings and bands of Indians weren't enough to contend with, outlaws had recently moved into the area along the Sweetwater River.

At about the same time, this young lad was assigned to carry a cash delivery along with his usual mail. So he took precautions, hiding the cash by covering his first mochila with a second one. He filled the pockets of this second mochila with worthless papers and set off on his ride.

As he entered the mouth of a narrow canyon, the young rider saw two horsemen approaching. Trapped by the steep canyon walls, he had no choice but to dismount when the two men drew their rifles. As one of the men reached for the mail pouch, the boy grabbed the other end and flung it up in the outlaw's face. He quickly shot the other villain. Then he leapt into his saddle, dug in his spurs, and rode right over the top of the first villain. So it was that young Billy Cody, later known as Buffalo Bill, made his escape into open country and carried the mail through.

No less heroic than Cody was "Pony Bob" Haslam. Once, when Indian raids had run off

"Pony Bob" Haslam

horses and riders at several relay stations, Haslam rode 380 miles (612 km) in thirty-six hours to fill in the gaps. In March 1861, Pony Express riders broke all previous records when they delivered a copy of President Lincoln's first inaugural address to California in seven days and seventeen hours. Of all the riders along the route, it was Haslam who recorded the fastest time. Even though an arrow had broken his jaw and bullets had shattered his arm during an Indian attack, Haslam completed the 120-mile (193-km) ride at an average speed of almost 15 miles (24 km) an hour.

Yet even with the kind of dedication exemplified by the likes of Cody and Haslam, the final days of the Pony Express were approaching. William Russell, in an effort to continue financing the mail service, had convinced a government official to lend him a large sum of money. But the loan was illegal, and Russell was arrested. His reputation would never fully

The transcontinental railroad would soon connect the eastern United States to the West.

recover from the blow. And without his support, it was unlikely that the Pony Express would continue much longer.

But even without Russell, the Pony Express seemed destined to be a short-lived experiment from the beginning. Following close on the heels of the young men who carried the mail to California and back, were laborers laying the tracks for a transcontinental railroad. With them came the telegraph. Completion of the cross-country telegraph on October 24, 1861, took away business previously handled by the Pony Express.

The Pony Express riders could not compete with the telegraph.

In November 1861, about a year and a half after its inception, the Pony Express made its last delivery. But, Pony Express riders would long be remembered for their accomplishments. They had carried 34,753 pieces of mail. They had traveled a distance equivalent to twenty-four laps around the globe. They had strengthened ties between the Atlantic Coast and the Pacific Slope, bringing them ten days closer together.

"A fast and faithful friend has the Pony been to our far-off state," wrote a newspaper editor in California. "Summer and winter, storm and shine, day and night, he has traveled like a weavers shuttle back and forth till now his work is done. . . . We have looked to you as those who wait for morning, and how seldom did you fail us. . . . Goodbye, Pony! . . . You have served us well."

Soon the big steam engines of the transcontinental railroad would haul the mail out to California and back. Back on April 3, 1860, before Johnnie Frye left St. Joseph and rode west across Kansas with that first batch of mail, Mayor Jeff Thompson shared these words with the crowd: "Hardly will the cloud of dust, which envelops the rider, die away before the puff of steam will be seen on the horizon."

The mayor was right. The West was changing fast. Like a rider on a mail route, the Pony Express would appear and vanish in a cloud of dust.

Even though the Pony Express was a short-lived endeavor, the hard work of its riders helped unite the rugged West with the rest of the nation.

GLOSSARY

counsel – advice

formidable – causes nervousness or fear

inaugural – relating to a ceremony in which a leader is installed in office

invest – to give money to a company in hope that the company will be successful

jeopardize – to risk failure; to place one's success in danger

lobby – to try to influence a public official

outpost – a branch of an organization that is separate from the main group

promoter – one who tries to bring success to a cause by spreading news of its value

spur – a pointed piece of metal worn on a horse rider's boot heel; when the rider "spurs" the horse (or kicks it with the spurs), the horse gallops faster

stagecoach – a horse-drawn vehicle that carried passengers and mail

stamina – the ability to stand up to harsh conditions

summit – the peak, or top, of a mountain

promoter

stagecoach

TIMELINE

1848 Gold is discovered in California; thousands of Americans head West

1850 California enters Union as a free state

1851 Chorpenning gets government contract to deliver mail between Sacramento and Salt Lake City

Senator Gwin introduces bill to establish weekly letter express to and from California **1855**

Gold discoveries in Colorado and Nevada bring more settlers to the West **1859**

1860

1861

April:
Pony Express is established

Transcontinental railroad completed **1869**

October:
Transcontinental telegraph line completed

November:
Last deliveries made by the Pony Express

INDEX *(**Boldface** page numbers indicate illustrations.)*

PHOTO CREDITS

©: Cover, Stock Montage, Inc.; 1, Pony Express National Memorial, St. Joseph, Missouri; 2, Wells Fargo Bank; 4, Harold Warp Pioneer Village Foundation; 5, TJS Design; 6 (top left), Utah State Historical Society. All rights reserved. Used by permission; 6 (top center), Denver Public Library, Western History Department; 6 (top right), Pony Express National Memorial; 6 (bottom left), Bettmann Archive; 7, North Wind Picture Archives, Hand-colored woodcut; 8, Pony Express National Memorial; 9 (top), Bettmann Archive; 9 (bottom), 11, North Wind; 12, 13, Bettmann Archive; 14, TJS Design; 15, Nevada Historical Society; 16, Bancroft Library; 17, UPI/Bettmann; 18 (top), Bettmann Archive; 18 (bottom), Scotts Bluff National Monument; 19, 20 (bottom), North Wind; 20 (top) Suzanne Clemenz Photography; 21, 22, Utah State Historical Society. All rights reserved. Used by permission; 23, North Wind, Hand-colored woodcut; 24 (top), Pony Express National Memorial; 24 (bottom), Bettmann Archive; 25, Denver Public Library, Western History Department; 26, AP/Wide World; 27, North Wind, Hand-colored woodcut; 29, Frederic Remington's *The Coming and Going of the Pony Express.* 1900. Oil on canvas, #0127.2333. From the Collection of Gilcrease Museum, Tulsa; 30 (top), Utah State Historical Society. All rights reserved. Used by permission; 30 (bottom), North Wind, Hand-colored woodcut; 31 (top right), Bettmann Archive; 31 (bottom right), North Wind; 31 (bottom left), AP/Wide World

ABOUT THE AUTHOR

Peter Anderson has worked as a river guide, carpenter, newspaper reporter, writing teacher, editor, and wilderness ranger. He has written twelve books for young readers on topics related to nature, American Indians, and the history of the American West. He has lived in Utah and Wyoming, not far from the route of the Pony Express.